LOCH NESS MONSTER
ENDURING MYSTERIES

KEN KARST

Published by
CREATIVE EDUCATION

P.O. Box 227, Mankato, Minnesota 56002
Creative Education is an imprint of The Creative Company
www.thecreativecompany.us

Design and production by Danny Nanos of Gilbert & Nanos
Art direction by Rita Marshall
Printed in the United States of America

Photographs by Alamy (Dale O'Dell), Corbis (Bettmann, Hulton-Deutsch Collection),
iStockphoto (FrankRamspott, Matt84, Vaara), Shutterstock (Thomas Ahlheim, Linda Bucklin, John A Cameron,
Circumnavigation, Janaka Dharmasena, Matthew Egginton, frantisekhojdysz, Antonio Gravante, Victor Habbick, Chris
Harvey, Mike Heywood, Eric Isselee, Ralf Juergen Kraft, Francois Loubser, martiapunts, Mechanik, Kovalchuk
Oleksandr, OSORIOartist, Pics by Nick, Pincasso, rangizzz, M Rutherford, scubaluna, Alexey Stiop),
SuperStock (De Agostini, Science Photo Library, Stocktrek Images)
Series logo illustration by Anne Yvonne Gilbert

Library of Congress Cataloging-in-Publication Data

Karst, Ken.
Loch Ness Monster / Ken Karst.
p. cm. — (Enduring mysteries)
Includes bibliographical references and index.
Summary: An investigative approach to the curious phenomena and mysterious circumstances
surrounding the Loch Ness Monster, from legendary sightings to exploratory sonar use to hard facts.

ISBN 978-1-60818-403-3
1. Loch Ness monster—Juvenile literature. I. Title.

QL89.2.L6K37 2014

001.944—dc23   2013036060

CCSS: RI.5.1, 2, 3, 6, 8; RH.6-8.4, 5, 6, 7, 8

9 8 7 6 5 4 3 2

CREATIVE EDUCATION

Table of Contents

November 12, 1933, was a fine day for a walk in northern Scotland. The sun was shining, and the winds were light. So Hugh Gray grabbed his camera and ambled down to the new road along the southeastern shore of Loch Ness, the long, narrow lake near his home. As Gray walked along, he spotted something unusual—what looked like a long, gray creature splashing in the water about 60 feet (18.3 m) from the shore. Gray quickly snapped several photos. Within days, the *Daily Record*, a newspaper in Glasgow, Scotland, had printed one of the pictures, accompanied by Gray's explanation that it was a 40-foot-long (12.2 m) beast with a submerged head and vigorously splashing tail. Gray's was the first photo of what soon became known as the Loch Ness Monster. But when some people looked at it, they saw only a branch floating in the water, or perhaps a dog swimming with a large stick in its mouth. In the eight decades since, there have been many more photographs, thousands of reported sightings, and several scientific searches. But the details of the Loch Ness Monster remain as blurry as whatever was captured in Gray's photo.

NESSIE COUNTRY

The **British Isles** is a land of storytellers. Honed in long hours spent by the fireside—fighting off the chill of the long northern nights or the damp of the sea air—the British tradition of storytelling has contributed legendary tales of saints and ghosts, kings and queens, heroes and fairies, and sailors and serpents to the world's literary culture. Many of the stories understandably involve the sea, which is never far from any point in the isles. There are stories of selkies, creatures who can change from seals to humans and back. Then there are kelpies—horses that can appear on a beach, offer a ride to a weary traveler, and then plunge into the deep, drowning the unfortunate **trekker**. And of course there are mermaids, creatures that are half-woman and half-fish, long believed by sailors to bring bad luck on a voyage.

The seemingly calm waters of Scotland's Loch Ness are home to centuries-old legends of a strange, quiet creature lurking in the depths.

But the best-known creature of them all may be the Loch Ness Monster, believed to live in the cold, murky, and mysterious depths of

the Scottish lake for which it is named. Popularly known as "Nessie," the monster is different from most other storied beasts in one important way: It seems to want to have nothing to do with people. And that only adds to its mystique. There have been thousands of sightings, but for the most part, Nessie has eluded photographers, filmmakers, **sonar** trackers, and other more sophisticated researchers. Though estimated at times to be as large as 40 feet (12.2 m) long, he or she has appeared more like a flash in the corner of one's eye—a dark, moving figure on or in the water, here now and gone an instant later, but far too big to be ignored.

Loch Ness is in northern Scotland, in a region called the Highlands. It's about as far north as the North American cities of Juneau, Alaska, and Churchill, Manitoba. But winters on Loch Ness are mild because of the Gulf Stream, a warm ocean current flowing across the Atlantic from the Gulf of Mexico to northwestern Europe. Temperatures in the Highlands

The Scottish Highlands' craggy valleys, formed by the same glaciers as Loch Ness, are rich in both geologic and folkloric history.

don't often drop below freezing, and Loch Ness rarely, if ever, freezes over.

The lake lies along the Great Glen **Fault**, which extends through northwestern Ireland and into the North Atlantic. The portion through Scotland measures 60 miles (97 km), from the Atlantic Ocean northeast to the North Sea. More than 400 million years ago, two large pieces of the earth's crust called tectonic plates came together but didn't quite fuse. The fault is where they abut, or touch, each other. Erosion along the fault caused the gap that is Loch Ness. Studies have shown that the rock in one of the steep walls of Loch Ness might be as many as 200 million years older than rocks in the other. The two plates below still rub against each other, causing occasional tremors—shakings of the earth that aren't quite as strong as earthquakes.

Loch Ness, in the northeast end of the Great Glen, is 24 miles (38.6 km) long but only 1 mile (1.6 km) wide. That might seem small for such a famous body of water, and if it weren't such a windy place with such changeable weather, the loch might offer an easy canoe paddle from one shore to the other. But its surface area makes it the second-largest lake in Great Britain. Loch Ness is extremely deep—745 feet (227 m) at its deepest point—and holds more water than any other lake in Great Britain. Geologists believe the bottom of Loch Ness is made of loose material deposited by glaciers during the last ice age, which ended more than 10,000 years ago, and that the material fills the bottom of a much deeper V shaped by the loch's steep walls.

Before the plates collided to form the Great Glen Fault, there was open sea above them. But as the land came together, it cut off Loch Ness from the sea. Some people believe that the Loch Ness Monster could be

descended from prehistoric sea creatures that were trapped as the plates shifted and the sea disappeared. Today, because the surface of the land has continued to rise since the weight of glaciers lifted, Loch Ness sits 50 feet (15.2 m) above sea level.

The rising surface caused the seawater to drain out of Loch Ness. Over time, it was replaced by fresh water from rain and the rivers flowing into the loch. That means that if Nessie's ancestors had been in the loch when it contained seawater, they would have had to **adapt** quickly to their new environment. Freshwater fish now live there, though the loch doesn't contain enough nutrients to support large populations. Those that swim there are cold-water species such as trout and salmon. In the summer, the temperature at the water's surface stays around 60 °F (15.6 °C)—uncomfortably chilly for people—and the deeper water registers about 42 °F (5.5 °C).

Because the weather in the Highlands is habitually chilly and damp, dead plants don't decay as quickly as they do in warmer climates. Instead, they form **peat**. The rivers that flow into Loch Ness carry so much peat that the water in the loch is brown. A person can see only about 5 feet (1.5 m) into it. That has made searching underwater in Loch Ness difficult. Not only is the brown water difficult to see through, but the peat particles reflect light from photographic flashes, so pictures taken underwater are often marred by bright streaks of light.

Indeed, if any creature wanted to hide from people, Loch Ness would be a good place to do it. Sunlight can penetrate only a few feet into the brown water, so most of the depths are extremely dark. People looking for Nessie in recent years have found, in various places on the lakebed, stone

Scotland's major industries include fishing (above) and whiskey, the latter of which makes use of peat (opposite) to fuel its malting ovens.

rings constructed by people who lived in the area just after the last ice age, similar to those at Stonehenge and dozens of other locations in Britain. They've also found a World War II bomber that crashed in 1940. But no evidence of a monster. Not even so much as a bone.

Does that mean that the Loch Ness Monster is just a story? Many scientists, and even those at the British Natural History Museum in London, have scoffed at the notion of a large, unidentifiable creature lolling about in a Scottish loch. But Roy Mackal, a retired University of Chicago biologist and a cofounder of the International Society for **Cryptozoology**, said he believes there is some sort of giant creature in Loch Ness. In the 1970s, he asserted that it was an **amphibian** but later changed his mind to say it was a whale-like mammal. He even presented drawings of **hypothetical** Nessies in his 1976 book *The Monsters of Loch Ness.*

Tim Dinsdale, who gave up his career in aeronautical engineering to live at the loch for a period in the 1960s, participated in several research efforts shortly before Mackal and also wrote a book about the monster. In *Project Water Horse*, he claimed there are plenty of reasons to believe in Nessie: "One can argue tediously about the pros and cons of scraps of evidence—of photographs, films, sonar-recording and their meanings—but if an **objective** view is taken and the facts concerning them are studied, and admitted, there is enough evidence already to establish reality." Dinsdale made that statement more than 35 years ago. But no one's found Nessie yet.

Take a Second Look Binoculars, a video camera, a boat, a sonar unit—all are important tools when it comes to sighting the Loch Ness Monster. But so is something called "expectant attention." Expectant attention is a psychological condition in which a person sees something unusual only because he has recently become aware that it might be there. Sightings of unidentified flying objects (UFOs) are frequently the result of expectant attention, and many sightings of Nessie might be as well, since people at the loch search harder for a monster than they might otherwise. A similar psychological **phenomenon** is pareidolia, or thinking that an abstract sound or image is something recognizable. Seeing faces in clouds, human figures in rocks, or animals in blots of ink are examples of pareidolia, in which the brain fits familiar details to something unfamiliar. So is hearing words in random noises, or fitting nonsense phrases to blurry rock-and-roll lyrics.

When a photographic image taken in 1975 beneath Loch Ness was said to possibly be the face of the Loch Ness Monster, it might have been pareidolia at work. Later explorers in the same area found a sunken log with a pattern on the end that closely resembled the image in the picture.

WHAT

IS

THAT

THING?

When people have said they've seen the Loch Ness Monster, just what is it they have seen? Sometimes it's a small head and long neck sticking out of the water, like a **periscope**. Sometimes it looks like a horse's head. Sometimes that figure is followed by several humps in the water—and certainly a large or thick body mass. Sometimes it's just a few humps moving rapidly through the water. Sometimes it has horns, or has a powerful tail and dives quickly. Sometimes it has even appeared on land, slithering, or moving on some short **appendages**. Its color is usually described as being dark gray, dark brown, or black, but sometimes it's lighter. And it's typically 20 to 40 feet (6.1–12.2 m) long.

When scientists want to make sense of such a wide range of evidence or ideas, they often use a reasoning strategy they call Occam's Razor. It's an approach that states, basically, that the simplest answer is probably the right one—or at least the best place to start. Occam's Razor is not the handiest strategy for those wishing to prove the existence of the Loch Ness Monster. Naturalists and others have said that instead of being a surviving relative of prehistoric creatures, the "monster" is far more likely driftwood

or other floating debris. Or, they say, it could be a trail of water left by a passing boat, since waves tend to bounce off the steep shores of the narrow lake and create unusual patterns and peaks on the water. Gordon Sheals, former zoologist at the British Natural History Museum, explained it this way: "The thing we call the Loch Ness Monster is really a mixture of many different things [which] could include rotting vegetable material, logs, tree stumps, tree roots, gases escaping from the bed of the loch, and commonplace objects which could be distorted by **mirage** effects."

Mirages have fooled many on Loch Ness, and they occur under the same conditions as Nessie sightings commonly do. In fact, quiet, windless weather is known around northeastern Scotland as "Nessie weather." Cool air is a powerful tool in making mirages, often causing distant objects to appear larger than they really are or stretch them upward. This can make small swimming creatures look as though they are much larger.

Another factor that can fool the eyes when looking at the loch is the water disturbance called a seiche (*SAYSH*), occasionally caused by heavy southwesterly winds that can blow the length of the loch. The wind pushes huge volumes of water to one end, and when it dies down, the water sloshes back with great force, creating underwater waves as high as 131 feet (39.9 m). These waves have registered on sonar screens looking somewhat like long, humpbacked monsters. On the water's surface, seiches can push logs and other debris against the wind itself, causing witnesses to believe they have seen a strong, swimming creature.

Even without the presence of mirages or seiches, other animals have been commonly mistaken for the monster. Harbor seals, which can swim into the loch through channels from the North Sea, are prime suspects,

Hundreds of millions of years ago, monster-like sea creatures swam in Earth's waters, some with flippers, tails, and elongated necks.

While some explain the sightings as seals (below), Nessie supporters look to prehistoric creatures such as plesiosaurs (opposite) for clues.

since they are often up to 10 feet (3 m) long. But seals are far more curious about people than Nessie and poke their heads above the water far more often, too. The animal most often taken for the Loch Ness Monster is probably the European otter, a long, sleek, thick-necked, short-legged animal that is at home both on land and in water. These otters can grow to 3 feet (0.9 m) long, not including their tails, so they're not huge. But they often travel in family groups, perhaps causing observers to mistake them for the humps of a monster.

Could Nessie have simply swum into the loch from the sea? That's unlikely. In the early 1800s, Loch Ness and other lochs in the Great Glen were connected by the construction of the Caledonian Canal, which allows large boats to pass from the Atlantic to the North Sea. But the canal has 24 steps to raise and lower boats between the varying water levels in the glen. It's hard to imagine that a sea creature the size of Nessie could have made that passage without being noticed.

But Mackal and other researchers insist that the people who have claimed to have seen a monster in Loch Ness can't all be wrong. Compiling similarities in what witnesses have described, they've concluded that Nessie could be an animal thought to have gone **extinct** millions of years ago—specifically, either a plesiosaur or a *Basilosaurus*. Plesiosaurs were long-necked, bulbous-bodied sea reptiles measuring about 60 feet (18.3 m) long, with small, horselike heads. But the **vertebrae** of plesiosaurs were so close together that it would have been difficult for them to flex their necks into the swanlike pose often ascribed to Nessie. Also, they were reptiles, whose fossil

remains are almost always found in warm water, not cold. (Reptiles are cold-blooded, meaning their bodies take on the temperature of their surroundings. They get very sluggish in cold environments.) Moreover, there hasn't been any evidence that plesiosaurs have lived anywhere in the world in the past 60 million years. If some had been trapped in Loch Ness, that would have had to have been after the last glaciers melted away, only about 12,000 years ago.

Mackal had originally thought that Nessie might be a plesiosaur, but he later came to believe it was a *Basilosaurus*. The size is about right. *Basilosaurus* was more alligator-like than plesiosaurs were, and it was also a marine mammal of the same order as dolphins, whales, and porpoises. Mammals are warm-blooded, which means their bodies maintain a constant temperature, usually warmer than their surroundings. Mammals also have to breathe air, so mammals that live in water have to surface often. But other ocean mammals surface more often than Nessie is believed to, and *Basilosaurus* was also apparently incapable of deep diving, something Nessie is thought to practice regularly. Additionally, *Basilosaurus* hasn't left any evidence on Earth for about 40 million years.

If Nessie is either of these creatures, it would have been a quite a trick of survival. It would almost certainly have to be part of a breeding population to have survived so long, but none of the sightings of the Loch Ness Monster has ever included smaller creatures that might be babies or juveniles. Researchers have theorized that the monster would require 20, 50, or as many as 500 of its kind in the loch to reproduce with the kind of **genetic diversity** needed to maintain a healthy population. Also, a 1993 project by the British Natural History Museum and the Freshwater Biological

As the largest animal of the Late Eocene period, the ancient whale Basilosaurus ("king lizard") stretched 40 to 60 feet (12.2–18.3 m) long.

Association determined that the entire loch is home to about 20 tons (18.1 t) of fish. That's enough to sustain only a single two-ton (1.8 t) Nessie. But estimates based on its size indicate the monster might weigh as much as 50 tons (45.4 t). There probably aren't enough fish—or plants, for that matter—in Loch Ness to keep Nessie fat, happy, and reproductive.

Most researchers also say it's unlikely that a large prehistoric creature could have continued to survive in Loch Ness without leaving more traces. But others note that a coelacanth, a large, bony fish believed to have gone extinct about the same time as the plesiosaurs (65 million years ago), was discovered off the coast of Africa in 1938. Why not a living fossil in Loch Ness?

The late-1990s discovery of a second coelacanth species near Indonesia reminded the scientific world of nature's unknown possibilities.

The Father of Cryptozoology

Bernard Heuvelmans (1916–2001) was a Belgian-French scholar who earned a doctorate in zoology. But mere zoology wasn't enough to sustain his interest in the natural world. He decided to research animals that were unknown to science or thought to have gone extinct. In 1955, he published the French edition of *On the Track of Unknown Animals*, which was translated into English three years later. His work provided the foundation for an entire field he himself later termed "cryptozoology," or the study of hidden animals. Heuvelmans applied traditional scientific methods to his research but also made allowances for **myths** and legends, which proved popular among the general public but made the scientific community skeptical of his work. His first book sold more than one million copies. His second book to be translated into English, *In the Wake of the Sea-Serpents*, covered the mysterious creatures of the seas, including the Loch Ness Monster. Heuvelmans visited Loch Ness in the early 1960s and expressed anxiety that he might actually see the monster. A Nessie appearance, he said, might be satisfying personally but could reduce his stature as a scholar, even among popular readers, by appearing too coincidental to be true.

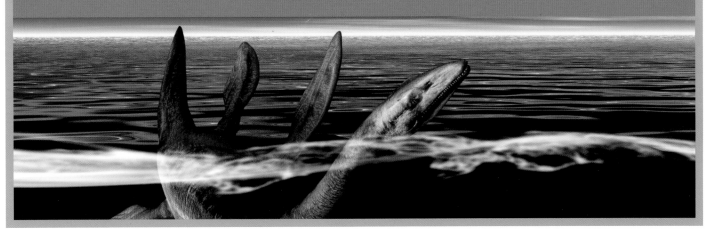

SEEING IS BELIEVING (AND RARE)

Starting as long ago as the sixth century A.D., when an Irish missionary named St. Columba ordered a monster to stop attacking a swimmer, there have been many stories of monster sightings in Loch Ness. But until the 20th century, the loch had been a remote place, so sightings were relatively rare. The soldiers who built the military supply road along the south side of the loch in 1715 reported seeing two creatures "big as whales." One story, published in *The Times* of London in 1856, involved tourists who'd gone looking for kelpies and instead encountered a 40-foot-long (12.2 m), eel-like creature. Another involved a farmer named Alexander MacDonald who was chasing a runaway lamb on the shore when a large beast emerged from the water, crawled up on land on stubby fins, and came within 150 feet (45.7 m) of him. In 1880, a different MacDonald, this one named Duncan, was diving to inspect a shipwreck near Ft. Augustus, at the southwestern end of the loch, when he emerged white and shaking with fear. It was several days before he could bring himself to tell of seeing a huge, frog-like animal perched on a rock shelf below the surface.

After a road was built around Loch Ness in the early 1930s, residents and tourists could drive around the entire scenic, mountain-ringed loch. Between April and October of 1933 alone there were 20 sightings, and there have been thousands since. About 10 sightings per year are considered possible monster sightings worth investigating, author and scholar Roy Mackal said. But he suspects that only a small fraction get reported because people are afraid of being ridiculed if they say they saw the monster.

The classic photographic image of the Loch Ness Monster shows a huge creature looking almost like an

Apatosaurus swimming majestically with its head high above the water atop a long, thick neck. The photo, credited to London physician Kenneth Wilson in April 1934, appeared in the *Daily Mail*, a popular London newspaper, and created a global sensation. But because there was no background in the photo, it was hard to gauge the relative size of the creature and the waves. Some researchers were suspicious. Sixty years later, the picture was revealed to have been a fake—a photo of an animal neck built atop a tiny model submarine, constructed to trick the *Daily Mail*.

Naturalist Adrian Shine, who in 1987 coordinated a sonar sweep of Loch Ness, brings a mix of skepticism and open-mindedness to Nessie. He described Tim Dinsdale's ideas that the loch's walls are full of caves where a monster might hide as "folklore." Shine and two other researchers examined a film in which Dinsdale had captured the monster apparently swimming and declared it had been a movie of only a distant boat. He continues to direct and

For years, the towering, herbivorous (plant-eating) Apatosaurus of the Late Jurassic period was incorrectly known as Brontosaurus.

29

publish research on the loch but gives some respect to the continuing random sightings by individuals. "Witnesses are not drunk and come from all walks of life," he says. "Almost all of them are wholly sincere." Most reports come from visitors and not residents, suggesting that the monster was not made up simply to attract tourists, he notes.

Nevertheless, one of the first highly publicized sightings originated with the manager of the Drumnadrochit Hotel on the north side of the loch. In the spring of 1933, Aldie Mackay, the hotel manager, and her husband John were driving along the shore of the loch when she spotted a whale-like creature out in the middle of the water. She kept quiet about it for several days, but soon the story got to Alex Campbell, a law enforcement officer at the loch, who wrote an article about the sighting for the *Inverness Courier*. His article, which was printed on May 2, 1933, used the term "Loch Ness Monster" for the first time.

That July, two Londoners, Mr. and Mrs. George Spicer, were driving along the south shore of Loch Ness when they saw a long, dark shape on the road about 600 feet (183 m) in front of them. As they approached, they saw an almost featureless but massive creature, nearly four feet (1.2 m) high. "An ugly creature," George Spicer called it. "Like a huge snail with a long neck." It was "loathsome," he added. "Horrible. An abomination."

The creature didn't appear to have a head or a tail. The Spicers, who later drew a picture of the creature, had never heard of the Loch Ness Monster. Later, some skeptics thought they'd simply seen an otter.

With each telling of the tale, the creature's size increased, from 6.5 feet (2 m) to 29 feet (8.8 m)! It was one of the last recorded encounters with the monster on land.

In 1960, Tim Dinsdale got the first motion picture images of the monster. He filmed it for 4 minutes as the creature swam away from him and then up the opposite shore at about 10 miles (16.1 km) per hour. Britain's Joint Air **Reconnaissance** Intelligence Centre determined that the image on the film was "probably an animate object." But two decades later, this was the film scrutinized by Shine and fellow researchers. They announced their findings—that the "monster" had been a boat obscured by glare—after Dinsdale's death in 1987.

In the late 1960s, after decades of failed attempts to gather evidence on the water's surface, researchers from universities and other scientific organizations armed themselves with advanced equipment and took their quest underwater. In August 1972, American inventor Robert Rines, director of the Academy of Applied Science in New England and a lecturer at the Massachusetts Institute of Technology, led a search involving sonar **synchronized** with flash cameras 120 feet (36.6 m) below the surface of Loch Ness. Two of the team's photos almost certainly showed a diamond-shaped flipper of some kind. At 6.5 feet (2 m) long, it was thought to have been part of an enormous animal.

Three years later, Rines returned to the site with photographers from both *National Geographic* and the *New York Times* and achieved dramatic results: one photo showed a bulb-bodied creature with a 15-foot-long (4.6 m) neck seeming to swim upward, and the other showed what appeared to

Researchers, tourists, and scientists alike have tried to prove (or disprove) Nessie's existence by capturing a definitive shot on film.

be a close-up view of a **gargoyle**-like face. The photos were printed in magazines around the world, and British naturalist Peter Scott stated the monster should have a scientific name: *Nessiteras rhombopteryx*, a Latin term meaning "Loch Ness creature with a diamond-shaped fin." But that term, and the photos themselves, were met with criticism from other experts who thought that the pictures had been enhanced. Questions arose about their authenticity. Some suggested the whole-body photo was actually an image of the bottom of Rines's boat. One Scottish politician even noted that if someone scrambled the words "Nessiteras rhombopteryx," one result would be "Monster hoax by Sir Peter S."

In 1987, Shine's "Operation Deepscan" used 20 boats in a line dropping what Shine called a "curtain of sonar" through the loch. They identified some kind of swimming creature, larger than a shark but smaller than a whale, but couldn't determine exactly what it was. Years of further exploration turned up nothing. In 2001, Rines traveled the length of Loch Ness 8 times, and in 2003, the British Broadcasting Corporation (BBC) sponsored a sweep involving 600 sonar beams, but both searches proved fruitless.

Monster? What Monster? A group of Scotsmen recently tried to convince the United Nations (UN) to declare Loch Ness and the Great Glen a World Heritage site. That would give it global recognition as having "outstanding universal value," along with such places as the Great Wall of China, the Statue of Liberty, and Grand Canyon National Park. Scottish leaders said the loch deserved recognition because it is one of the most significant natural features in Great Britain, because it played an important role in Scottish history, and because it features the Caledonian Canal, an engineering marvel built between 1803 and 1822 and still in operation. The canal, which connects Loch Ness with several other, smaller lochs, was built to allow boats sailing the Atlantic Ocean and the North Sea to cut through Scotland instead of having to sail around it. But the group seeking the special status for the Great Glen specifically left out any mention of Nessie in its application, even though the monster is known around the world. A Scottish tourism expert said the loch needed to broaden its appeal beyond the "myth" of the monster. The UN hadn't awarded the special designation as of 2013, but the effort to earn it was ongoing.

AS SEEN
ON
YOUTUBE

One mystery about the Loch Ness Monster is why it's so famous, considering that there are "similar" monsters thought to be frolicking in 300 lakes around the world. The United States and Canada claim several such creatures. Tucked among the ski hills, dairy farms, and forests of Vermont and upstate New York, Lake Champlain seems an unlikely residence for a sea monster. But reports of a long, serpent-like creature poking above the lake's surface, and sometimes even crawling ashore, extend from American Indian tales to YouTube videos. The French explorer for whom the lake is named, Samuel de Champlain, is sometimes said to have seen Nessie, though he might have been remarking on the great numbers of large fish. In 1873, some railroad workers along the shore reported seeing a serpent with an enormous head approaching them from the lake. Within days, there were reports of livestock that were killed and dragged into the water.

Nearly a century later, a Connecticut couple picnicking with their children near the lake snapped a picture of a huge animal with a small head, long neck, and humped back about 150 feet (45.7 m) away. Some researchers determined that the apparently legitimate photo showed a creature that was unidentifiable except to say that it was likely to be

Some say other animals are behind the Lake Champlain sightings, but a 2005 fisherman's video may have recorded an encounter with a plesiosaur-like creature.

24 to 78 feet (7.3–23.8 m) long. Cryptozoologists suggested that the creature, like Nessie, could be a *Basilosaurus*, whose ancestors might also have swum into the lake when it was part of the Atlantic Ocean and been trapped there when the land rose and isolated the lake. Other researchers believed it might have been a log, tossed upward by a seiche. In any case, today the monster is known as "Champ," a friendly sea creature that is even the mascot of the minor league baseball team in Burlington, Vermont.

Canada's version of Nessie is known as Ogopogo. According to legend, Ogopogo lives in Lake Okanagan, a 69-mile-long (111 km), 3-mile-wide (4.8 km), 750-foot-deep (229 m) lake in British Columbia. Ogopogo is said to have special powers and is even credited with the ability to control the weather. Unlike the gods of old, who unleashed rain and lightning but were never seen, Ogopogo has been sighted—and recently. In 2004, a family sleeping aboard a houseboat on the lake was awakened by a thumping on the boat. John Casorso grabbed a video camera and recorded what looked to be a 15-foot-long (4.6 m), slimy, greenish-black animal with several humps swimming about 50 feet (15.2 m) away. It swam off, and then sank below view. Others have described the monster as being brown or green, with a head like a snake's, or a cow's, or a horse's. Its length has sometimes been

estimated as 70 feet (21.3 m), while the number of humps it has shown while swimming across the water ranges from 1 to 4. If the idea that Ogopogo has a horse's head (even a mane) and a forked tail is widespread in Canada, it's probably because that's how an artist presented it on a Canadian postage stamp in the 1990s.

One of the Great Lakes, Lake Erie, which stretches west-to-east with Ohio and Pennsylvania on its south shore and Ontario on its north shore, is said to contain a monster known as South Bay Bessie. Bessie has been regularly sighted by Great Lakes sailors and visitors since the 1790s. In 1998, a family at Huntington Beach, west of Cleveland, Ohio, spotted a disturbance in the water about 500 feet (152 m) offshore. Bubbles gave way to a long ripple, and then to three black humps, which appeared to be part of a moving, living creature. Or could it have been driftwood, or boat wakes, silhouetted by the setting sun? Or a seiche, a common occurrence on Lake Erie, as on so many others? As with Nessie, each sighting creates more mysteries.

Rines, whose expeditions captured the controversial Loch Ness photos in 1972 and 1975, suggested a new theory about Nessie in 2008: the creature could have fallen victim to **global warming** and died. Of course, the

Mysterious sightings of large, serpentine creatures have been reported around the world in freshwater lakes, ponds, and reservoirs.

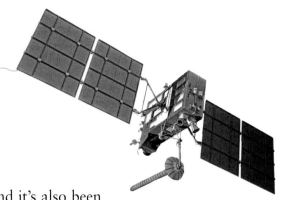

water in the loch remains cold, particularly down deep. And it's also been warming ever since the glaciers began melting at the end of the last ice age, when some believe Nessie's ancestors might have been trapped in Loch Ness. But the idea is one explanation for why Nessie hasn't been identified.

Meanwhile, new technology continues to be developed that could help researchers get a look into some of the darkest corners of Loch Ness. Sonar and GPS, which uses satellite signals to target precise locations on the globe, continue to be combined in ways that make underwater searches far more accurate. And research groups such as the Woods Hole Oceanographic Institution (WHOI) have developed new tools for searching places as deep as the ocean floor. For example, WHOI used torpedo-like probes equipped with sonar and cameras and guided from the surface of the Pacific Ocean to search an area at the bottom of the ocean in 2006. The effort to locate the plane of aviator Amelia Earhart, who disappeared in 1937 while trying to become the first woman to fly around the world, was ultimately unsuccessful. Nessie seems to be similarly elusive, as it has thus far managed to avoid some of the most aggressive searching and sophisticated imaging technology ever assembled.

It's possible that if Nessie were ever found, a little bit of magic would be lost. Would people look at the loch in the same expectant way? Without a mystery, would Nessie hold the same attraction it does now? What would happen to the hundreds of books and the handful of films and documentaries that have been made about the monster? Some have speculated over the years that Scottish officials wanted to keep the legend of Nessie alive as a way of bringing tourists to Loch Ness. If the monster were identified, or if it has died, would the ruined castle on the shores of Loch Ness and

Some mysteries—from Amelia Earhart's disappearance to the Loch Ness Monster—may never be solved, despite technological gains.

A cormorant can look like a miniature Loch Ness Monster because of the way it swims with its head and neck protruding from the water.

the spectacular scenery surrounding it make up for the loss of the mysterious monster? How would the Loch Ness Centre and Exhibition Experience, a popular attraction at the loch featuring research watercraft, interactive exhibits, photography, and history, survive without its starring character?

On the other hand, what if there has never been a monster? Could all those sightings over the centuries really have been just so many otters or boat wakes gleaming on the loch under a playful sun? Or could Nessie really be just a group of cormorants—long-necked, diving, duck-like birds? It would take a powerful trick of light and air and imagination, though, to turn cormorants, which range in size from about 18 to 40 inches (45.7–100 cm) long, into a 40-foot-long (12.2 m) water monster.

Yet some researchers have recognized that, while the odds are against Nessie's turning up, science is required to consider possibilities. It's a farfetched notion that a massive beast could have survived in a Scottish loch millions of years after its relatives vanished. It also strains belief that a creature so large could be hunted by so many for so long in such a narrow slip of water and not be found. But as long as Nessie remains a mystery, people are likely to keep pursuing it. Said Shine, "Whether the answer will teach us more about nature or about ourselves remains to be seen."

A Tragic Claim to Fame John Cobb was the world's master of speed. In 1939, he drove a car 367.91 miles (592 km) per hour, faster than any person had ever traveled on land. He outdid that record 8 years later, streaking 394.19 miles (634 km) per hour at the Bonneville Salt Flats near Wendover, Utah. When Cobb, who had been a pilot in Britain's Royal Air Force during World War II, wanted to take his need for speed to water, he went to Loch Ness. The world record for speed on water was 178.4 miles (287 km) per hour when Cobb brought his jet-powered boat, nicknamed "Crusader," to long, narrow Loch Ness in September 1952. For 3 weeks, he tested the 31-foot (9.4 m) aluminum and plywood boat over the mile (1.6 km) he was required to travel. On September 29, on calm water, Cobb exceeded 200 miles (322 km) per hour but then hit a mysterious wave. His boat disintegrated, and Cobb was killed. Many were quick to blame the Loch Ness Monster. But the true cause was attributed to wakes from Cobb's own support boats. The remains of Cobb's "Crusader" were found in 2002 beneath 656 feet (200 m) of water.

Field Notes

adapt: find new ways to survive in a changing environment

amphibian: a cold-blooded animal that can live both on land and in water

appendages: parts or organs joined to a body's trunk

British Isles: a group of islands separated from the coast of northwestern Europe by the North Sea and the English Channel; they include Britain, Ireland, and other, smaller islands

cryptozoology: the study of reports and other evidence of animals unrecognized by most scientists

extinct: no longer existing; usually said of a large group of plants or animals, rather than an individual

fault: a crack in the earth's crust

gargoyle: a carved ugly or distorted figure, usually a demon or animal, on a building

genetic diversity: a range of characteristics in a species that allow it to survive by adapting to changing environments

global warming: the phenomenon of Earth's average temperatures increasing over time

hypothetical: supposed, uncertain, subject to proof

mirage: an illusion caused by light passing through air of different temperatures, such as the appearance of water on a hot surface

myths: traditional stories that try to explain how something came to be or involve people or things with exaggerated qualities

objective: unbiased and relying on facts and observations; not influenced by emotions or personality

peat: brown, partially decayed plant material that can be dried and used for fuel

periscope: a device designed for observing from a concealed position, such as under water or around a corner

phenomenon: an occurrence that can be observed

reconnaissance: a search for useful military information

sonar: a technique using sound waves to navigate, find, or communicate with other objects under water, derived from the words "sound navigation and ranging"

synchronized: operated at the same time or rate

trekker: a person on a long or adventurous journey, usually on foot

vertebrae: the individual bones that make up the spinal column

Selected Bibliography

Clark, Jerome. *Encyclopedia of Strange and Unexplained Physical Phenomena.* Detroit, Mich.: Gale Research, 1993.

Delrio, Martin. *The Loch Ness Monster.* New York: Rosen, 2002.

Dinsdale, Tim. *Project Water Horse: The True Story of the Monster Quest at Loch Ness.* London: Routledge and Kegan Paul, 1975.

Emmer, Rick. *Loch Ness Monster: Fact or Fiction?* New York: Chelsea House, 2010.

Landau, Elaine. *The Loch Ness Monster.* Brookfield, Conn.: Millbrook, 1993.

Mackal, Roy P. *The Monsters of Loch Ness.* Chicago: Swallow Press, 1976.

Meredith, Dennis L. *Search at Loch Ness: The Expedition of the New York Times and the Academy of Applied Science.* New York: Quadrangle/ New York Times, 1977.

Shine, Adrian. *Loch Ness.* Inverness, Scotland: Loch Ness Project, 2006.

Websites

LEGEND OF NESSIE

http://www.nessie.co.uk/htm/searching_for_nessie/search3.html

Read up on eyewitness accounts, biographies of researchers, and an updated list of sightings.

LOCH NESS AND MORAR PROJECT

http://www.lochnessproject.org/index.htm

Access the research archive, Young Loch Ness Explorers' page, and analyses of photos of "sightings."

Index